BURR RIDGE, IL 60521

CUTTING A RECORD IN NASHVILLE

CUTTING A RECORD IN NASHVILLE

BY LANI VAN RYZIN
Photos by the author

Franklin Watts
New York/London/Toronto/Sydney/1980
A Triumph Book

To Clyde and Nancy

Library of Congress Cataloging in Publication Data
Van Ryzin, Lani.
  Cutting a record in Nashville.

  (A Triumph book)
  Includes index.
  SUMMARY: Text and photographs record the steps involved in cutting a record in Nashville, one of the nation's top recording cities.
  1. Phonorecords—Juvenile literature. 2. Sound recording industry—Tennessee—Nashville—Juvenile literature. [1. Sound recording industry—Tennessee—Nashville] I. Title.
TS2301.P3V36   789.9′1   79-24816
        ISBN 0-531-04114-X

R.L. 3.8 Spache Modified Formula

Copyright © 1980 by Lani van Ryzin
All rights reserved
Printed in the United States of America
5 4 3 2

Introduction

1

Music City, USA

6

How a Record Begins

10

Inside a Recording Studio

14

Studio People

26

At a Recording Session

31

Other Types of Recording Sessions
48

Mixing and Mastering
51

Pressing the Record
64

The Record's Final Stop
73

Recording Terms
78

Index
83

CUTTING A RECORD
IN NASHVILLE

Introduction

About one hundred years ago, the only sounds you could hear were those that were being produced at that very moment. Today, we can fill the air with stored-up sound. Records and tapes preserve sound in a permanent form. They can be played back any time we wish. Sounds can be heard that were made in faraway places or long ago.

Even before a method of storing sound was discovered, people were using music-making machines. Most of these worked like music boxes on wound-up springs. The one pictured here used a cylinder that had little bumps on it. Whenever these bumps hit the metal keys, they made a sound. As you turned the crank, which turned the cylinder,

An early music-making machine.

different bumps hit different keys to make a song. By putting different cylinders on the machine you could play various songs.

Even though these machines made music, they did not play recorded music. The songs you heard were being made each time you turned the crank.

One of the first disc machines was a disc-playing music box. Giant brass discs had patterns of tiny tabs sticking up from their surface. The disc rotated on a machine with teeth. As each metal tab hit a tooth, it made a sound. The pattern of different sounds determined the song.

But this was still not recorded music. It was music being produced each time the disc was played.

Sound creates waves that travel through the air. In 1877, Thomas Edison discovered that these waves could be stored in solid form as patterns. These patterns could then be played again and again, at any time. At first, Edison used a cylinder wrapped in thin tinfoil to preserve the sound. A metal stylus (needle) was then attached to a diaphragm—a tight drumlike skin. When a sound was made near the diaphragm, the air waves from the sound would make the diaphragm vibrate. This

A *disc-playing music box*.

made the stylus, which was placed on a cylinder, vibrate too. When the cylinder was made to rotate, the vibrating stylus would cut grooves in the tinfoil. Later, when the stylus was run over the same grooved cylinder again, the diaphragm would vibrate in the same way, and thus produce the same sound.

After Edison, many inventors raced to find new and better ways to preserve sound. Flat discs soon became very popular. In a short time, recorded music became big business.

Techniques of recording sound have continued to improve over the years. Today's stereo records give an almost live feeling to the sound they store.

The photos and information in this book tell about making records in Nashville. But the process is very much the same wherever records are made.

Music City, USA...

Nashville is often referred to as Music City, USA, and the name fits. Around fifty years ago, a Nashville radio announcer introduced a local country music broadcast as the "Grand Ole Opry." The name caught on and so did the music. Country music lovers across the nation became fans of the radio show. They came to Nashville by the hundreds, then by the thousands, to watch the show being broadcast. The stars of the Grand Ole Opry became national heroes and heroines.

As the popularity of the Opry grew, music publishers and recording companies from all over started coming to Nashville to set up shop. The music industry there grew by leaps and bounds. Today, it is one of the nation's top recording cities.

Though its roots are strictly country, Nashville's sound is changing. Its mild Tennessee climate, lush rolling hills, and small-town atmosphere have attracted all kinds of musicians. Even some who were trained at famous schools have come to Nashville. They prefer it to the rush and confusion of New York or Los Angeles. Today you can find a broad range of musical styles in Nashville. Everything from rock and rhythm and blues to disco, jazz, and classical music is being recorded there. Also, more and more television sound tracks are being produced in Nashville.

But even with its sound changing, country music is still king in Nashville. Local stores feature sequined jeans and satin spangled clothing for country performers. Cowboy hats and denim suits are displayed in shop windows. Thousands of tourists continue to file yearly through the Country Music Hall of Fame. There they see Elvis Presley's Cadillac, Minnie Pearl's hat, costumes worn by many of the all-time country music greats, and much more.

*In Nashville you can find
a broad range of styles.*

On the outskirts of town is sprawling Opryland Park. This park serves as a showcase for current stars and, with colorful displays, recreates for tourists the musical memories of the past.

As a recording center, Nashville attracts many singers and musicians who want to be stars. The Nashville bus depot is the stepping-off point for many star-struck hopefuls. Typically they come with a pack over one shoulder and a guitar over the other, hoping to find work in Music City, USA.

But the chances of making it big are very slim. Far more than luck is involved. It helps to have talent, persistence, the ability to work hard, and a knack for being in the right place at the right time. Many disappointed singers head home after years of trying to break into the Nashville music scene.

How a Record Begins

Records are produced for different reasons. Well-known musical groups and solo artists usually make recordings on a fairly regular basis. These records are financed by a major label and released nationally. Some groups produce their own albums or even have their own recording studios.

Unknown musicians or singers may cut a demo (demonstration record) to show what they can do. They will circulate it wherever they can. Usually, the musicians or artists themselves pay for these records. Only a small number of copies are made if the record is a demo.

Single records, mostly 45s, may be cut for beginning artists to test them on the public. These are circulated to hometown disc jockeys in hopes of getting some local support. They may also be sold from the stage during musical performances. If the record takes off locally, it may then be heard by a larger audience. Eventually this could lead to a contract with a producer or a major label.

Songwriters who want to sell a song may have studio artists and musicians record a demo of their song. This can then be presented to a song publishing company. Often songwriters just submit the written music to the publisher. However, if the publisher wants the song for its files, it may provide the money to have a demo made.

A group looking for new music can browse through a publisher's files and listen to the demos kept there. Song publishing houses keep track of who is looking for music and which artists have upcoming recording sessions. They usually know what type of music certain artists like and can make suggestions when new songs come in.

Many of the commercials you hear on radio or on television are recordings. Studio musicians and

Records or demos begin in a recording studio such as this one.

artists are usually hired to do these. The results are not sold as records, but instead are taped and then given to the various radio and television stations.

Whether a recording is a demo, a single for a new artist, an album for a well-known group, or a commercial, the steps involved in making it are all very much the same. And it all starts in a recording studio.

Inside a Recording Studio

Most of Nashville's studios are clustered in an older neighborhood, along what is known as Music Row. Here, you can find an almost endless stream of studios, housed either in trim modern buildings or in old remodeled homes.

Some of the finest studios with the most sophisticated recording equipment can be found inside remodeled bungalows. Many of these don't even have signs to show that a studio is located there. Musicians park in the driveway, pet the dog that's sitting on the back porch, and then go inside. The recording area may be set up in a room that was once a living or dining room. This homey atmosphere gives the studio a casual feeling—a relaxed setting for work.

Basically, there are two main areas in any recording studio. These are the studio room, where the musicians record, and the sound control room, which we will hear more of later. The two sections are separated by a glass wall. Sound engineers in the control room and musicians in the studio can talk to each other through mikes and earphones. An intercom system picks up the voices in each room.

The studio room is designed to be as soft and absorbent to sound waves as possible. In a room with hard walls and hard floors, sound waves can bounce around. This creates echoes and thin, tinny sounds. For a good recording the sound must be clear. This is why studios usually have carpeted floors. Walls may also be carpeted or covered with padded fabric, soft wood paneling, or drapes. Even music stands may be carpeted so that the sound of pages being turned won't be picked up on the mikes.

In a good recording each instrument is picked up only by its own mike. Studios try to prevent "bleedthrough," or sound being picked up by the

The studio room.

The sound control room.

Even music stands may be carpeted to absorb unwanted sounds.

wrong mike. For example, the mike in front of the guitarist should not be picking up any sound from the bass player. Ideally, the sound waves coming from a guitarist, or from any player, should drop flat about a meter away from him or her. This means the studio must be set up so that the musicians are spread out.

Drumbeats are difficult to control in this way. Therefore, the drums are always set up in a special soundproof booth. The drummer is positioned so that he or she can see the other musicians play. But the sound of the drums is picked up only by the drummer's mike.

The other musicians are spread out in the studio. Sometimes padded wall sections on wheels, called baffles, are moved around to create sound barriers between instruments. The vocalist is usually in a soundproof booth just big enough for a mike, a music stand, and a stool.

For the crisp, brilliant sound that can be produced by instruments such as strings or brass, a hard surface is necessary. Some studios have a tiled area with hard walls for when strings or brass are used.

Baffles can be moved around to create sound barriers between instruments.

The sound engineer can control what the musicians hear through their earphones. He or she can tune them in to what the others are playing and can adjust the volume so that each musician can hear the group as a whole. If someone wants to hear more bass or less drums, for example, the engineer can take care of this.

Small home tape recorders have only one track. You speak into one mike, your voice is recorded, and then you can play it back. Most large recording studios use a twenty-four-track recording system. In such a system there can be up to twenty-four separate mikes picking up different parts of the music and putting them all on one tape. This means that twenty-four separate layers of sound can be sandwiched in to make one blended sound. The tape used in such systems is about 2 inches (10 cm) wide.

Each track can be listened to separately. Any combination of tracks can be listened to together. If the sound engineer is not pleased with one of the tracks, he or she can "punch it out"—erase it.

Most songs are recorded in stages. Basic instruments may be recorded first. Each instrument is

The studio's twenty-four-track recording system.

recorded on its own track. Some instruments, such as drums, may have several mikes picking up the sound. When the instrumental tracks are finished, the lead vocalist may record on a separate track while listening through earphones to the instruments. Later, after the lead has been worked out to everyone's satisfaction, the backup vocalists, or harmony, may be added. At this time, the producer or songwriter may decide that bongos would sound good in a certain section of the song. These can then be added on another track. In this way, by juggling diffcrent combinations of tracks, music producers and arrangers can get just the blend of sound they want.

Suppose there are only two violinists in the studio and the producer wants to get the effect of a full violin section. This can be done. The violinists first record their parts. Then, listening through earphones so that they can keep the same tempo, they play their parts again on another track. This could be repeated any number of times. In this way, two violins can be made to sound like a dozen or more. Adding another musical part to what has already been recorded is called overdubbing.

The console, or control board, for the studio's recording system.

The sound control room is just that. It is the room where the sound is controlled. The control board for the twenty-four-track recording system is called a console. There are twenty-four rows of knobs, one row for each of the tracks. The knobs control many different sound effects. Dials above each row show the strength of the sound coming in on each track.

Studio People

Many different people are involved in a recording session. Producers finance the record. They may rent the studio, pay the studio musicians, and promote the record when it's finished. Most producers get a percentage of the profit. This percentage is agreed upon in a contract that is signed before the record is made.

Studio managers usually own the studio. They rent it out by the hour to various producers. Some producers own their own studios.

An arranger may write music or take a song someone else has written and adapt it. Arrangers may be hired by the producer to work on songs that have been selected for recording artists.

Studio musicians are hired separately by the producer. They are given the music when they arrive at a recording session. They must be capable of playing the music through in polished form after only a few brief trials. Even well-known musical groups rely on studio musicians to fill out the sound on their recordings. Many studio musicians play several instruments. This makes them valuable to the producer, who may want to overdub different instruments on different tracks.

The soloist or lead vocalists are called artists. Members of musical groups are also called artists.

The sound engineer (also known as the control, recording, or mixing engineer) runs the recording system and usually works for the studio. He or she is responsible for all of the technical aspects of the recording session. The producer and arranger often sit near the sound engineer during a session to direct the action.

Cartage companies are hired for storing and hauling instruments. Studio musicians usually use their own instruments. This means a lot of moving around from studio to studio for different recording sessions. Often a group will have the cartage com-

The storing and transporting of instruments is often left to a cartage company.

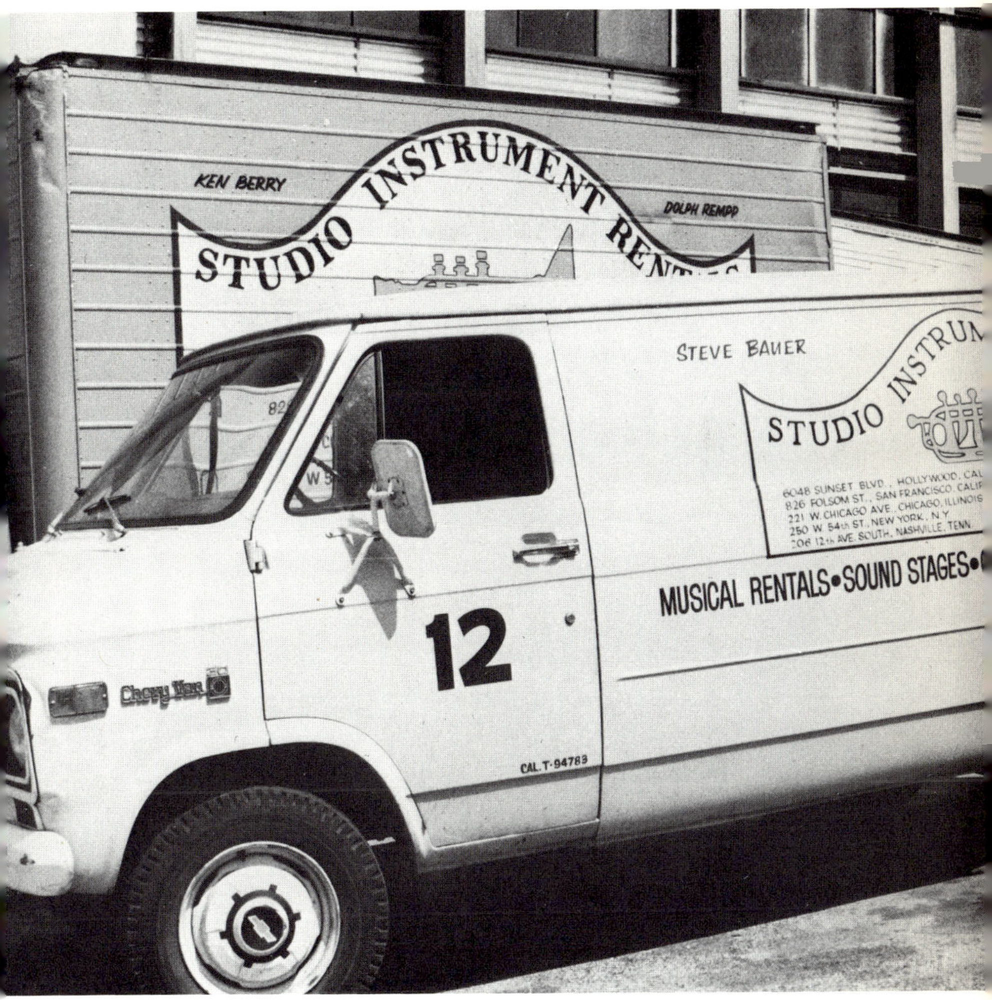

KEN BERRY
STUDIO INSTRUMENT
DOLPH REMPP
STEVE BAUER
STUDIO
6048 SUNSET BLVD., HOLLYWOOD, CAL
826 FOLSOM ST., SAN FRANCISCO, CALIF
221 W. CHICAGO AVE., CHICAGO, ILLINOIS
250 W. 54th ST., NEW YORK, N.Y.
206 12th AVE. SOUTH, NASHVILLE, TENN.
MUSICAL RENTALS•SOUND STAGES•
12
Chevy Van
CAL. T-94783

pany store its instruments in special protective cases between sessions. The instruments are delivered, set up, then hauled away after each session. The group simply calls and gives the company its recording schedule. When the musicians arrive at the studio, the instruments are there and ready. After the session is over, the instruments are again returned to storage.

At a Recording Session

Donna McElroy is going to cut a record. It will be a single—her first record to be released nationally.

Donna has been singing all of her life—at school, in church choirs, with Bible singing groups of all kinds, and then with several rhythm and blues groups in Nashville. Her voice is both powerful and tender at the same time. Her clarity of feeling draws you into the song.

Sanchez, a producer, heard her sing. He felt that with the right song and the right arrangement, Donna could make it as a top recording artist. The two have spent a lot of time together writing music and taping songs.

Donna majored in music in college. She now works as a counselor at a hospital. But she spends every free moment writing, singing, and recording music. She only does original music. Donna feels that once a song has been recorded there is no sense in doing it again.

Today's session will last all day. Its goal—to record Donna's first single. Before the session begins, Donna talks with Sanchez about her song.

It's hard to say who wrote the song. Donna, Sanchez, and several friends each worked on different parts. When something sounded right, they kept it.

"Songs sort of grow by themselves," says Donna. "Someone gets a melody going in their head. Someone else picks up on it and starts trying new things. We keep changing it, experimenting, and suddenly it begins to sound right." But even up to the last moment of recording, changes are still being made.

In the studio, Clyde, Tony, and Dave, the musicians, listen to a tape Donna has made of her song. They jot down their parts as they listen.

Very little music used in Nashville recording

Donna talks with her producer, Sanchez.

While they wait for the session to begin, Dave, Clyde, and Tony listen to a tape of Donna's song.

sessions is formally written out. A quick, musical shorthand based on do re mi as 1 2 3 is used instead. This number system allows the musicians to change the pitch of the song without rewriting it. Listening to a melody, they can quickly jot down numbers that stand for chords. If the singer later decides to do the song in a different key, they can change the key without changing the numbers.

Many musicians interpret and arrange their own parts. Once they've done so, they run through the song a few times together. Then they're ready to record.

Each instrument must be tuned. Here, inside the drummer's booth, Clyde tunes up using a key to tighten the drumhead. Note the strips of tape placed on the drumhead. These prevent a ringing overtone that could get picked up by the mikes.

In the control room, the sound engineer checks the studio mikes. Each track has a dial that shows the strength of the sound coming through. After all the instruments have been checked for sound, the recording session can begin.

The first take will record just the basic instruments—keyboard, drums, guitar, and bass. After

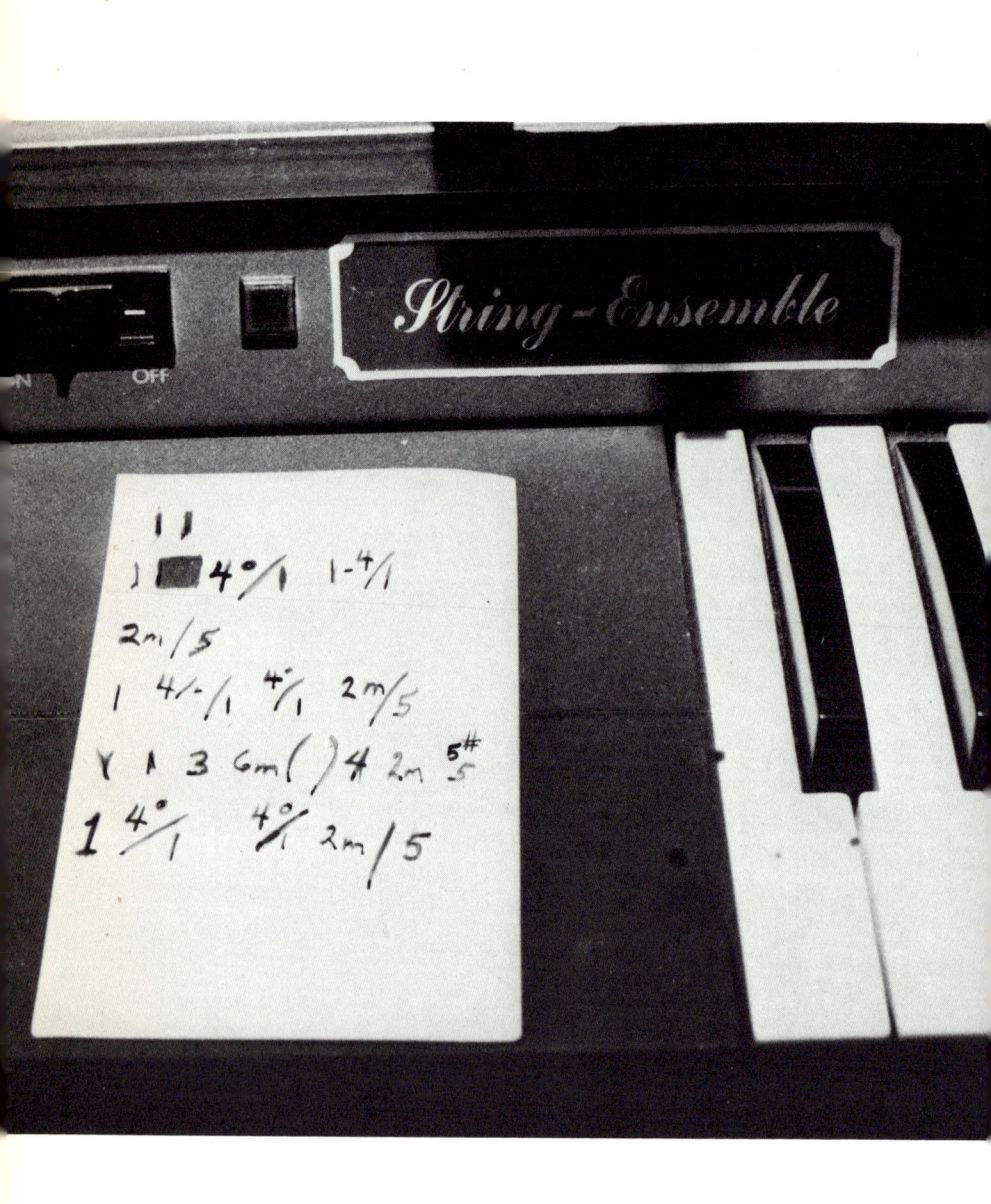

*A quick, musical shorthand saves musicians
time if they have to change keys.*

*The drummer, Clyde, uses
a key to tighten the drumhead.*

*The sound engineer
check the studio mikes.*

the first run-through, Donna and Sanchez discuss the tempo with Lloyd, the keyboardist. They all agree—pick it up a bit.

After a few more starts, they finally decide on one they like. They've now got a good take on instruments.

During a break, Donna works out one section of the song with Terry, the percussionist. "How about changing the pitch and repeating the main theme?" she asks. They try many different styles and tempos before finding one that works. "That's it," she says.

They've been working hard all morning and everyone decides it's time for a lunch break. One noble volunteer runs out to a fast-food place and returns to a hungry crowd. Chow time! The musicians, singers, and engineers all picnic in the control room and joke about the goof-ups of the day. Soon, with energy restored, they're ready to work again.

Back in the control room, Donna prepares herself mentally. They're ready now for her to record.

The instrumental track is fed to her through

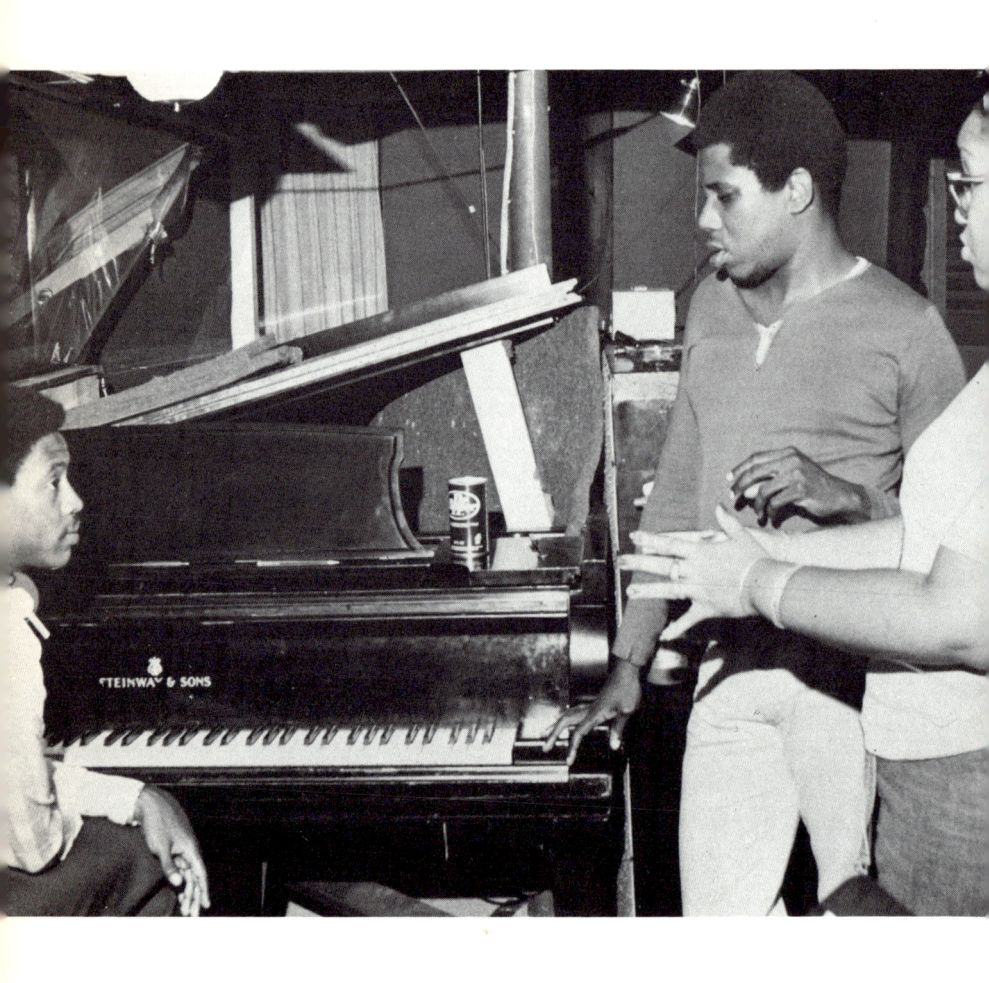

*Above: Donna and Sanchez
talk with Lloyd,
the keyboardist.
Right: Terry, the percussionist,
talks with Donna about possibly changing
the pitch in one section of her song.*

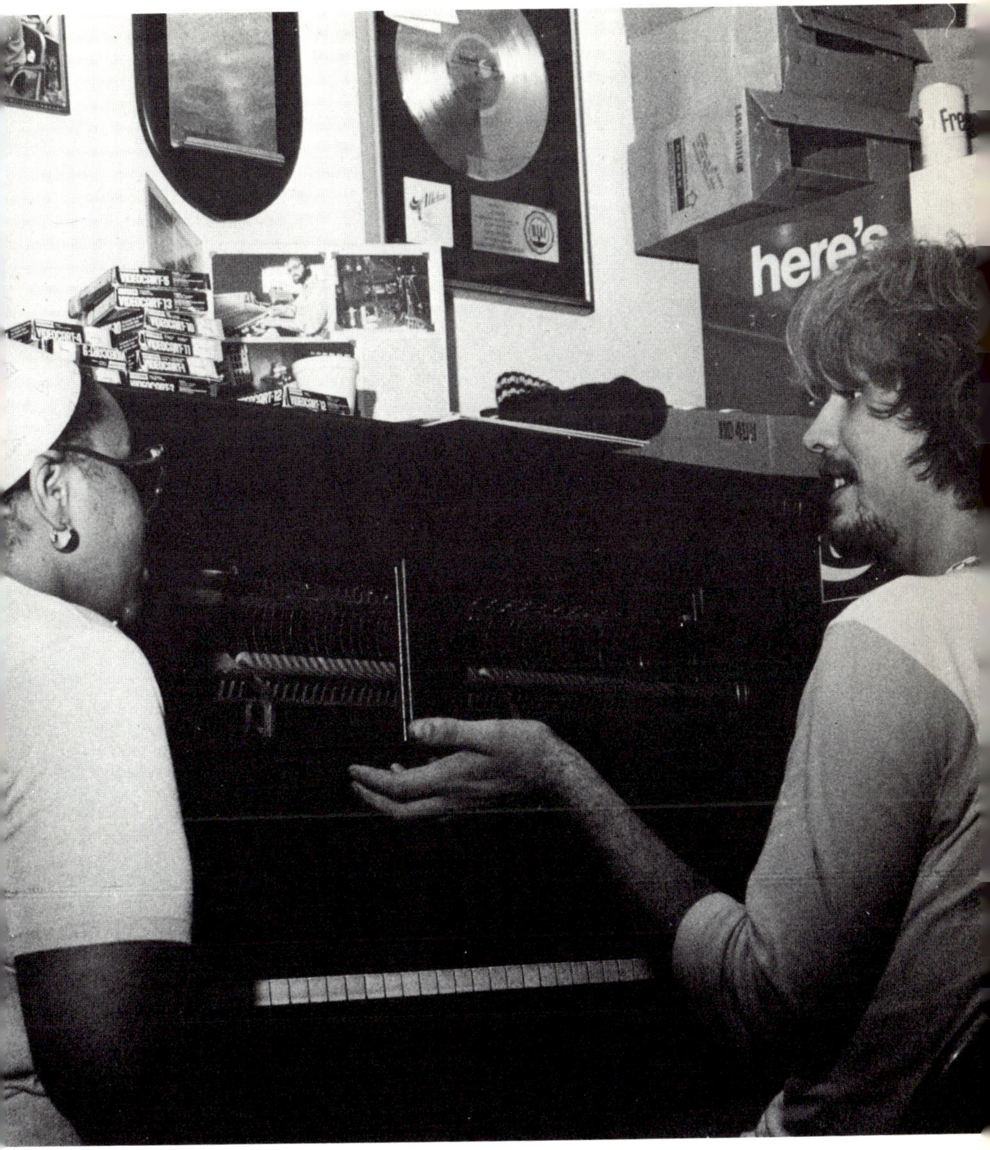
here's

the headphones. She listens and sings along. The other musicians stand by.

Donna is not happy with the middle section. She asks the engineer to punch it out. Then she sings along again to her own recording, and when she reaches the middle section, the engineer punches her in. Using this punching in and punching out method, Donna can repeat any section of the song she wants.

After an hour of taping, listening to the tape, and punching in sections, Donna is satisfied. Sanchez is too.

With the instrumental and lead tracks finished, backup vocals are next. Donna joins three other vocalists to do the harmony. Listening to the completed tracks on the headphones, the group informally warms-up. They try out different harmony parts with the lead. After a few different versions, Sanchez hears one he likes and says, "Let's go with that." They tape it.

Now basic instruments, lead vocals, and harmony are all on tape. Everyone listens to the combined tracks. All agree it needs more percussion. Marimba, congas, and bongos are recorded on three

*Donna sings along as she listens
to the recording of the instrumental track.*

Above: the group warms up for the taping of the harmony.

Marimba (above right), bongos, and congas (below right) are recorded on separate tracks.

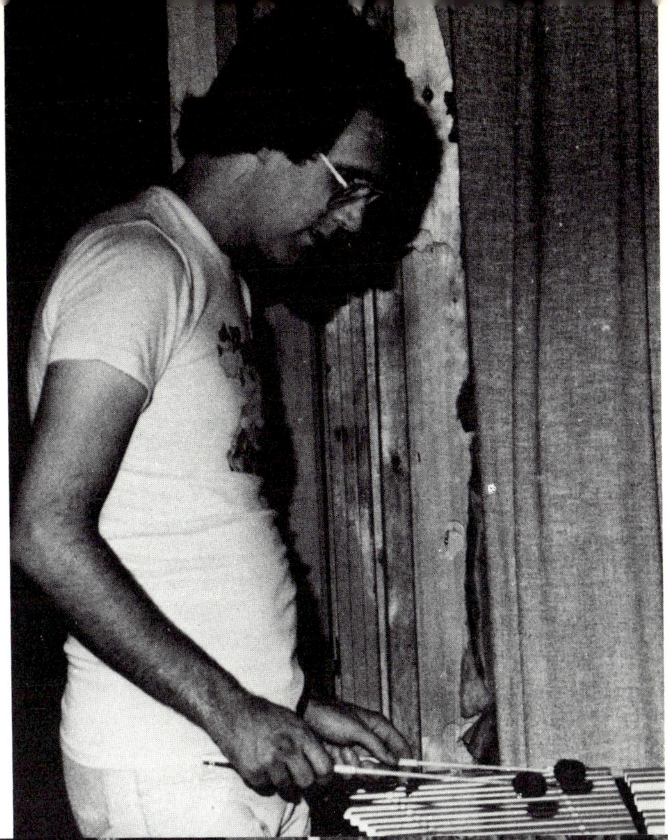
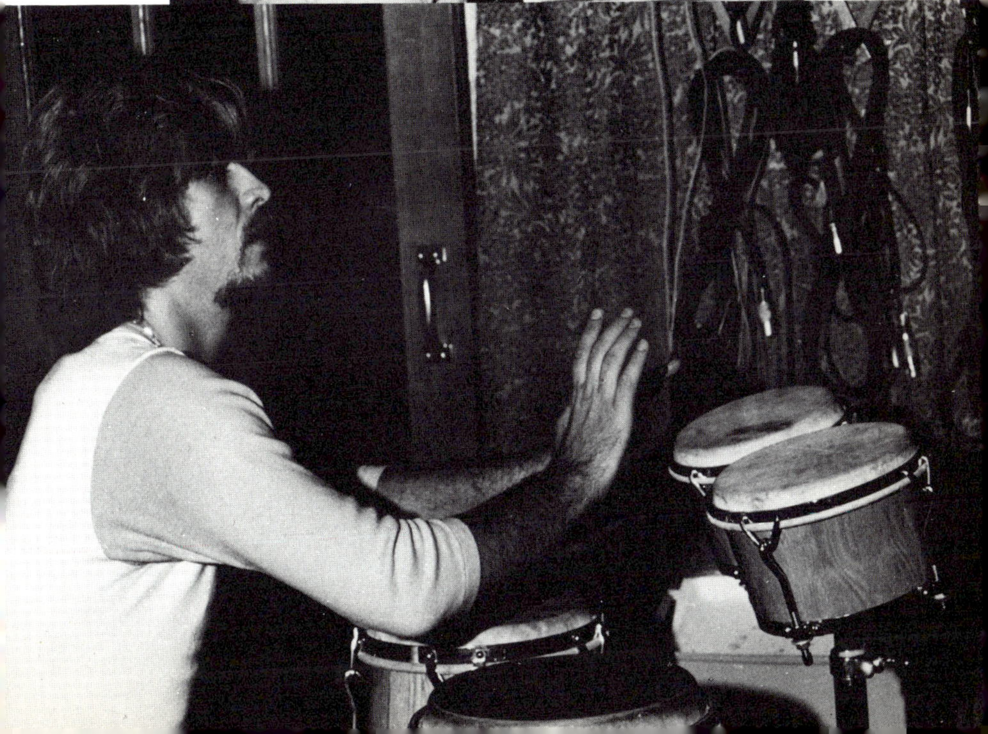

*The producer listens
to the finished tape.*

additional tracks. This gives them a selection of percussion tracks to choose from, though none of them may be used in the final blending.

The session is over! Everyone feels exhausted but pleased. Recording the song has been a full day's work. But listening to the finished tape makes it all seem worthwhile.

Now the waiting begins. It may be several months before Donna's record is ready for release. With luck, some radio stations will agree to play it. With more luck, it may take off. Meanwhile, Donna knows she will have to push on, working up another new song for yet another recording session.

Other Types of Recording Sessions

Some recording sessions are "live." In these, instead of recording various instruments on different tracks and overdubbing, all the instruments are recorded while playing together.

For a full orchestra sound, live recording is best. It would be difficult to record each instrument separately. In this case, a conductor directs the musicians and the group plays together for the recording. Mikes are set up around the studio to balance the sound.

In a live session overdubbing is still possible. After listening to the orchestra's sound on tape, the producer may decide that more violins are needed. The violin section may then tape their part

A "live" recording session.

on another track a second or third time, to fill out the violin sound. Sometimes, orchestra bells are added on a separate track. This gives the producer a chance to have two versions of the same music—one with bells for a holiday spirit and one without.

For commercials, exact timing is critical. The sponsor pays for only so many seconds or minutes of air time. Music recorded for commercials must be the exact length specified—down to the last second! Often this means picking up the tempo or slowing it down. As a result, some commercials must be taped many times before they are right. Spoken messages may be overdubbed on another track after the music has been recorded.

Mixing and Mastering

When the producer is satisfied that each sound track is good enough to go into the final record, he or she is ready to mix. Mixing is adjusting the sound on each of the tracks so that just the right blend is heard.

Each of the twenty-four tracks has been separately recorded. This means that each track can be played alone or any combination of tracks can be played together.

The producer, usually with the sound engineer, runs the twenty-four-track tape through the console. Each track has its own set of controls to regulate the sound. There are many effects that can be introduced at this point. Phasing creates a swirling effect, as though the sound were going round

*Many effects can be added as
a tape is run through a console.*

and round. A harmonizer can electronically add an extra sound a few notes off the main sound. Reverberations give a quivering sound to the music. Each knob in the track line controls the sound on that track in a different way.

The producer will play a song through many times, each time making small adjustments to different tracks. Many studios have a special mixing console that is separate from the console used in recording. The studio sound system has large, powerful speakers. If the producer wants to hear what the blended sound will be like on a home stereo, there are special speakers for that.

When the sound is blended and mixed it is recorded again on a standard-sized (¼" or .625 cm) tape. This is called the master tape. The wide, twenty-four-track tape is stored away.

When the master tape is completed, it is taken to a mastering plant. Here, the tape will be used to cut a master disc.

The mastering engineer plays the tape. He or she can adjust the volume or bring up the bass or treble. This is called equalizing. No other changes can be made in the music at this point.

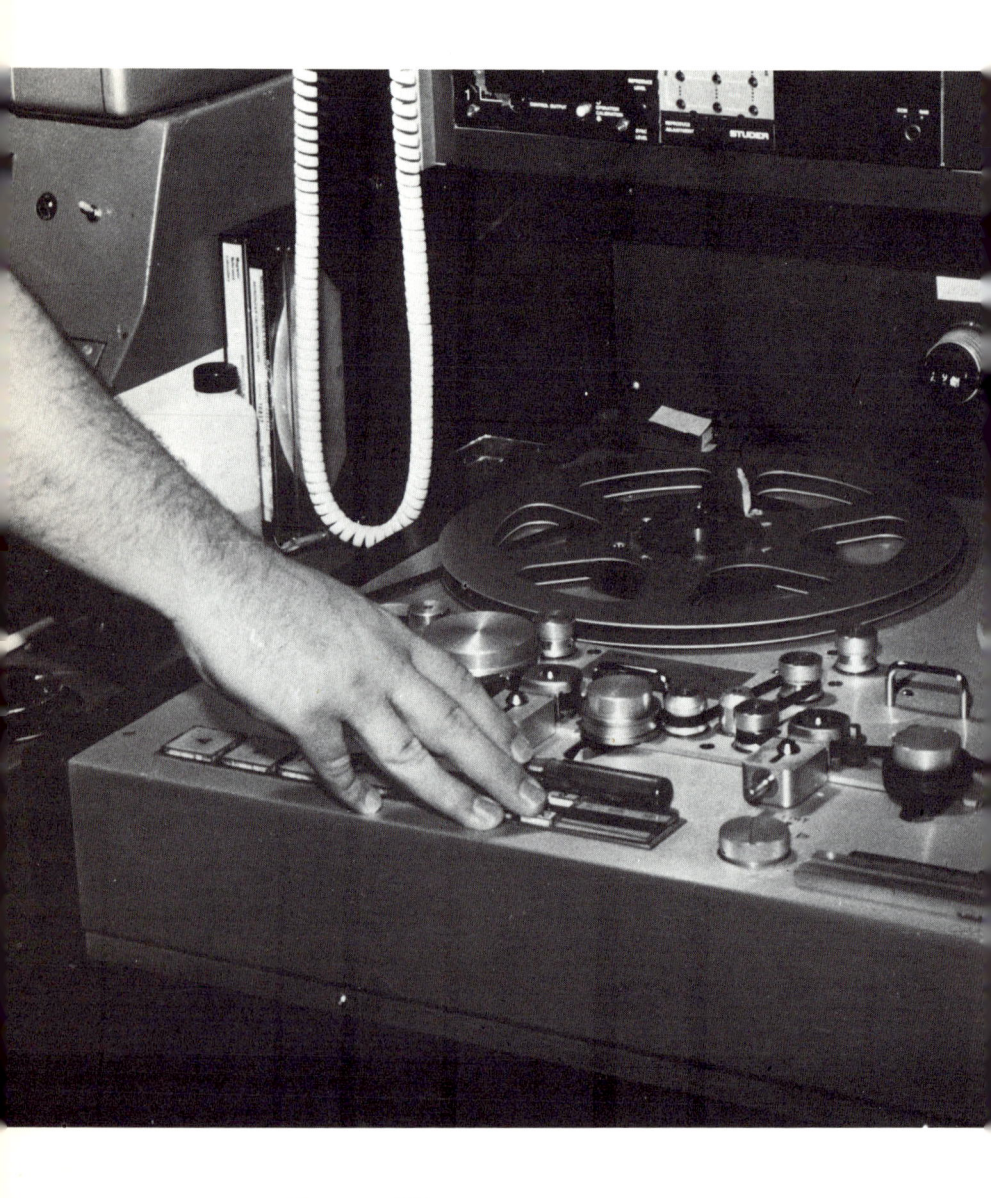

The master tape.

The mastering engineer equalizes the sound.

A blank disc, or lacquer, will be used to preserve the sound. The lacquer is a metal core disc covered with acetate. A disc-cutting machine, called a lathe, will cut sound grooves in the lacquer. To cut cleanly into the acetate, a sharp cutting stylus is used. Usually it is made of sapphire.

When the sound from the tape is played into the machine, it will be picked up as vibrations by the lathe. The vibrations cause the stylus on the lathe to vibrate also, cutting different shapes in the walls of the groove. When the record is played back, the stylus of the record player will follow the different shaped grooves and play back the same sound.

If you looked at a record's grooves through a microscope, you would see a spiral of wiggly channels. Each sidewall of the channel has a different contour to it. When you play a record at home, your stylus follows the spiral of grooves while the record turns. As the stylus touches the grooves, it passes over the different contours. This makes the stylus vibrate. The phonograph changes these vibrations back into sound—the same sound that was cut into the master disc. Wide contours in the groove make the stylus swing wide, creating deep,

*A disc-cutting lathe.
The lacquer is on the right.*

*Above: the lacquer being
cut by the stylus.*

*Right: a view of record grooves,
as they might be seen
through a microscope.*

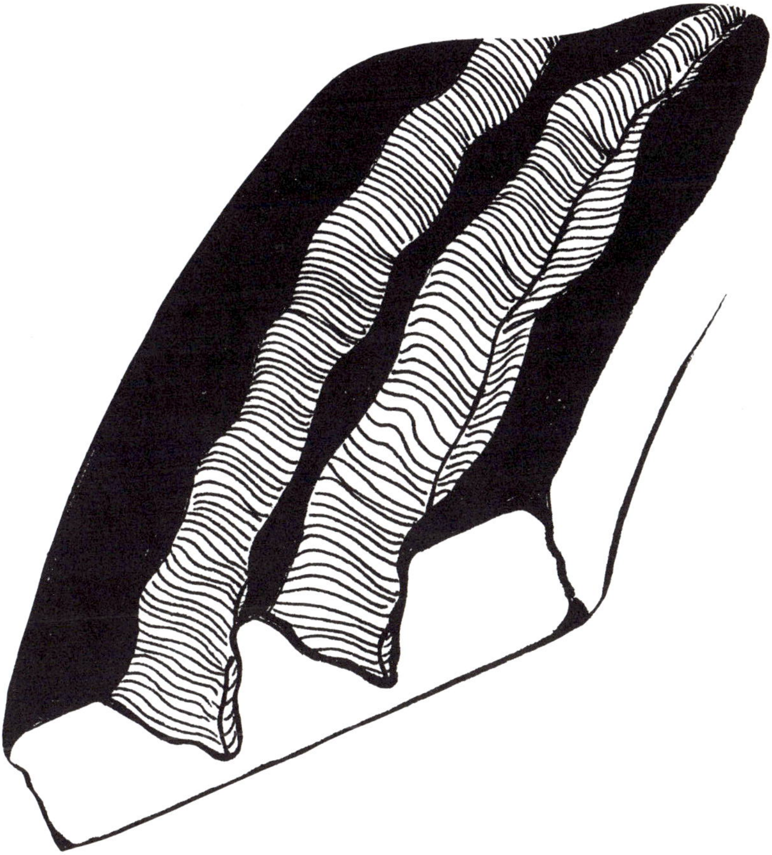

low sounds. Short tight contours in the grooves move the stylus in short patterns, creating high-pitched sounds.

The engineer listens to the tape. Volume is adjusted to just the right level. The engineer should be familiar with the music so that he or she can be ready to fade out the ending.

Now everything is ready. The lacquer is placed on the lathe and the tape is turned on. As the lacquer rotates, the stylus cuts the grooves. Using a microscope, the mastering engineer checks to see that the grooves are being cut cleanly, for a clear sound. Ragged cuts would create unwanted noise on the record.

During the mastering, the engineer checks from time to time to make sure the grooves are clean. As the song nears its ending, he or she gets ready for a fade out. The ending must not be snapped off too quickly nor the stylus be allowed to continue to cut after the song ends. If for some reason the engineer is not happy with the grooves or with the ending, he or she may decide to cut a new lacquer. A clear, uncluttered sound is a must. Every record made will sound just like this disc.

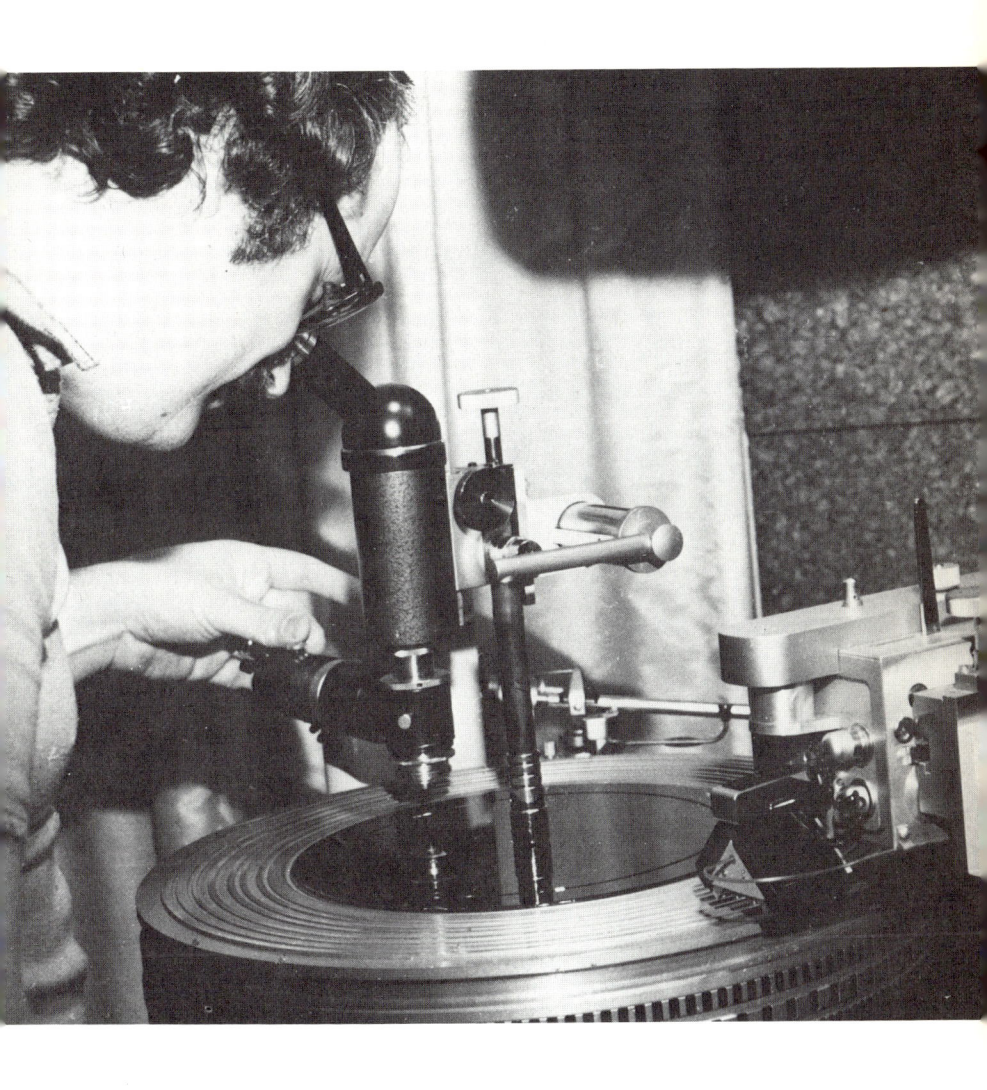

*The mastering engineer checks
to see that the grooves
are being cut cleanly.*

*A lacquer ready to be sent
to a processing plant.*

A separate lacquer is cut for each side of the record. Though the lacquer can actually be played a few times, it is not sturdy enough to be used often. Its main purpose is to preserve the sound.

Once the lacquers are ready they are sent to a processing plant. Here they will be used to make a negative mold in metal. This mold is called a stamper. It will be used to stamp, or press out, numerous copies of the record.

Pressing the Record

There are many separate parts to the record you buy at a record shop. For example, there is the label, the protective envelope, the album cover, and the plastic record itself. Artists and photographers are hired to design the album. They may also design posters and promotional advertising pieces at this time.

The paper parts of an album—the label, the envelope, and the album cover—are printed at a fabrication plant. The pressing plant receives all the separate parts, presses the record, and ships out finished boxes ready for sale.

Records are made from vinyl pellets that look like shiny lumps of tar. These are stored at the

The fabrication plant.

Vinyl pellets, which look like lumps of tar, are used for making records.

pressing plant in a tall silo and fed through chutes to pressing machines.

The metal stampers that were molded from the lacquer are fitted into a pressing machine. One stamper is used for each side of the record. The vinyl pellets are fed through the chutes to the machine. Here they are melted into a soft, round blob. This blob of melted plastic is then sent out of the melter on a spindle. Two labels, one for the top side of the record and one for the bottom side, are suctioned off a stack of labels. The labels are placed sandwich style, one on the top and one on the bottom of the melted blob. This sandwich is then fed into the pressing machine between the top and bottom stampers.

A fast heating and cooling action takes place as the blob is pressed between the stampers. The heat melts the plastic further, so that it fills all the grooves of the stamper molds. The cooling sets the plastic, making the record firm.

Some excess plastic oozes out of the stampers during the pressing and sticks to the rim of the record. As the record is fed out of the machine, this plastic is trimmed off. The completed record falls

The pressing machine.

*Labels are suctioned off
from their individual stacks.*

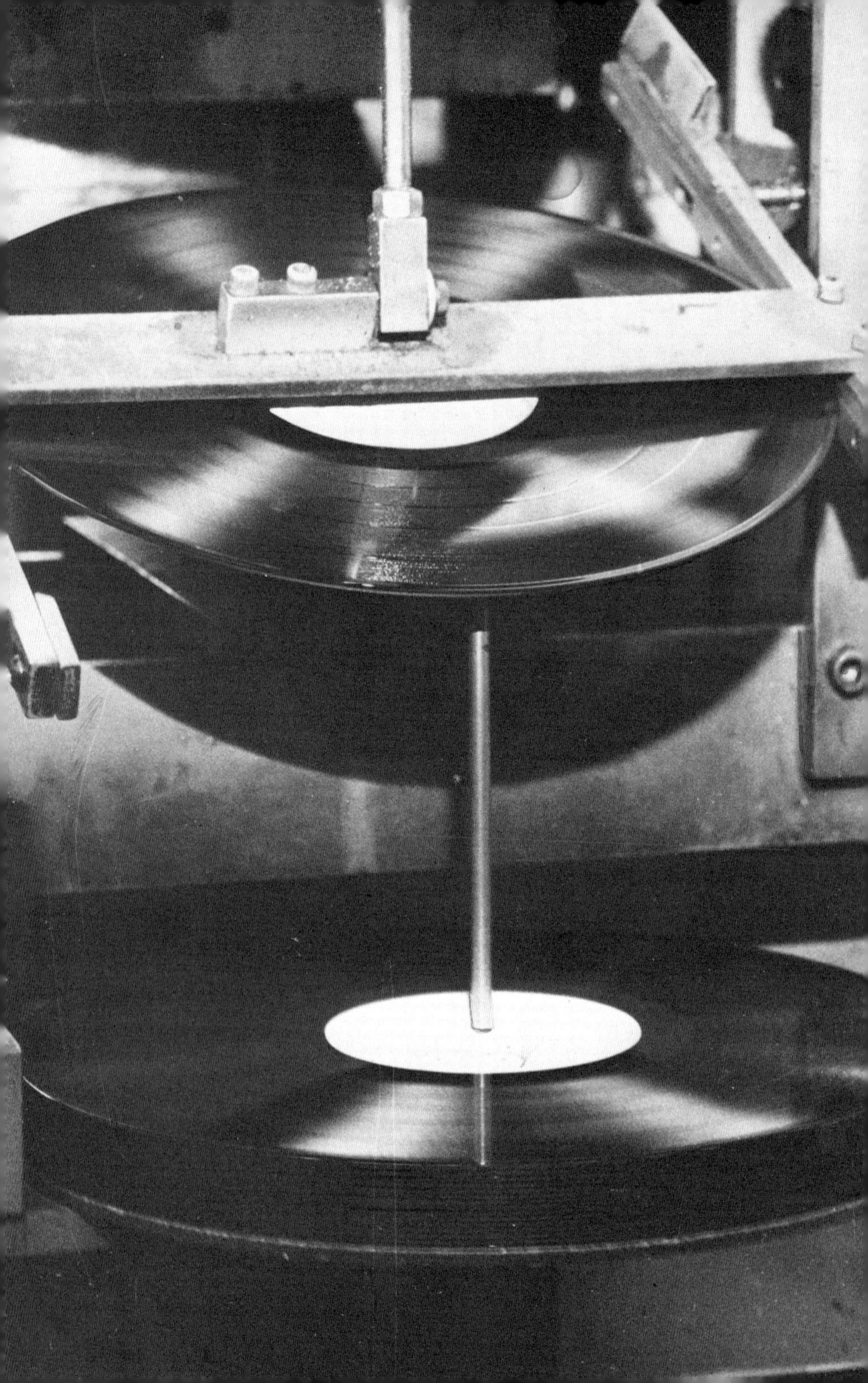

*Left: the trimmed record falls
onto a holding spindle.*

*Above: records are slipped
into album covers by hand.*

onto a holding spindle, where it will await the packer. The trimmed plastic edges are melted and used again.

Each record is slipped into an envelope and then into an album cover by hand. Next, the albums are carried over to another machine. Here they are fed between thin sheets of wrapping plastic. The plastic is cut and heated. This heating shrinks the plastic around the album, making a tightly sealed covering. The completed albums are then packed in boxes for shipping.

The Record's Final Stop

Often new records are first heard on the radio. Disc jockeys receive many free records from record companies. The DJ and the radio station decide what songs will be played and make up a stack of records called a rotation. This rotation is aired regularly by that station. Unpopular songs are dropped and new ones are added frequently.

You may hear a song you really like and decide to shop for it. Lists of new recordings and catalogs of long-time favorites are mailed to record shops by producers and record companies. Record shops order records from many different companies. Posters and display signs are also sent to shop owners to promote the sales of new albums.

When a new shipment of records is received, they are sorted into groups according to type of music—jazz, country, rock, rhythm and blues, and so on. Within each group, the records are arranged in alphabetical order by the artist's name. This makes it easy to quickly find a specific record, or just browse through your favorite type of music.

The money you pay for a record is divided up among many people. Some of these are the artists, the musicians, the songwriter, the producer, and finally, the shop owner. Other people receive a portion of the profit also. These include the studio engineers, the album photographers and artists, the printers, the pressing plant, and the advertising and marketing agencies.

The record you buy has been through many steps in its preparation. First, the sound was preserved on tape. Then, separate tracks were recorded. Other tracks were overdubbed, and all the separate sounds were then mixed and put on a master tape. Next, a master disc was cut. This disc was then used to make molds of the record, called stampers. Vinyl pellets were then melted and pressed between the

*Thanks to the record shop's
careful arranging, it is easy to find
the record you want.
Or you can just browse through
the section containing
your favorite kind of music.*

As you take the record from its cover and put it on your turntable, you become the first to hear sound come from it.

stampers, filling each groove in the mold to make your record.

As you unwrap your record and put it on your turntable, you become the first to hear sound come from it. Yet you know that what you are hearing is an exact copy of the sounds preserved in the recording studio.

It is important to treat your record gently. Keep it and your needle free of dust. Little pieces of dirt or oil can distort the tiny contours in the record's grooves and alter the sound.

And providing good, clear, true-to-life sound is what the recording industry is all about.

Recording Terms

The following are some of the terms used by people in the recording industry. They all appear in the text of this book.

Arranger   A person who alters music, puts it into a new style, or orchestrates a musical piece.

Artists   Soloists, lead vocalists, or members of a musical group.

Baffle (also called Gobo)   A wall section or partition used in a studio to separate instruments and their sounds.

Bleedthrough (also called Leakage and Crosstalk)   Sound leaking through to the wrong mike; each instrument's sound should be picked up only by its own mike and should not "bleedthrough" to another mike.

Console The control board for the recording or mixing system with adjustment knobs for each sound source.

Control room The room next to the studio from which much of the sound is technically controlled.

Demo A demonstration tape or record.

Earphones (or Headphones) A set of small speakers worn on the head. Through the earphones a person can hear what is being said in the control room or can listen to music fed into them by the engineer.

Equalizing Balancing the trebel (highs) and bass (lows) in the sound.

Fade Out The technique of gradually decreasing the volume of the music, usually done at the end of a song.

Label A recording company.

Lacquer An acetate disc with a metal core; grooves are cut in the lacquer in the recording process.

Lathe The cutting machine that uses a sapphire stylus to cut sound grooves in a disc.

Mastering Cutting a master disc, or lacquer, from the master tape.

Mastering engineer The person responsible for cutting the sound grooves in the lacquer.

Master tape The standard size (¼ inch) tape of the final blend of sounds recorded.

Mixing Adjusting the sound on each recording track to get the right blend.

Overdubbing Adding extra music to what has already been recorded.

Pressing The process of making copies of a record by squeezing melted vinyl between two molds.

Producer The person who sponsors a record. The producer usually sits in on the recording session and makes the final decisions.

Punching in Recording a new take over a previously recorded section. If a change is desired on a track it is not necessary to do over the whole tape. The recording engineer can punch the record button just before the section that is to be changed and begin a new recording on top of the old.

Punching out Stopping the tape from rolling; removing a section of a taped recording.

Rotation   A group or set of records selected by a radio station for regular airing.

Sound track   An audio tape for TV programs, commercials, or motion pictures.

Sound engineer   The person responsible for the recording equipment during a taping session.

Stamper   The metal mold made as a reverse imprint of the lacquer. The stamper is the mold used in pressing the records.

Stereo   The reproduction of sounds from the directions in which they were recorded.

Stylus   Commonly called a needle. A stylus is used in either cutting or playing a record.

Take   During a taping session, each performance that is recorded is called a take.

Track   The sound recorded from one sound source. There are often twenty-four separate tracks of sound that can be recorded.

Index

Air time, 50
Album cover, 64, 71
Arrangers, 26, 35

Backup vocalist, 23, 42
Baffles, 19–20
Bleedthrough, 15

Cartage company, 27–30
Commercials, recording, 50
Conductor, 48
Console, 24, 51
Country music, 6–7
Country Music Hall of Fame, 7

Demonstration record, 10–13
Disc jockey, 11, 73

Disco, 7
Disc-playing music box, 3–4
Drums
 recording, 19, 23, 35
 tuning, 37

Earphones, 21
Edison, Thomas, 3–5
Equalizing, 53

Fabrication plant, 64–65
Fade out, 60

"Grand Ole Opry," 6
Guitars, recording, 19

Harmonizer, 53

Instruments, tuning, 33

Jazz, 7

Labels, 11, 64, 67, 69
Lathe, 56–57, 60

Master disc (lacquer), 53, 56, 58, 74
Master engineer, 55–56, 60–61
Mastering, 53, 60, 63, 74
Mastering plant, 53
Melody, 32, 35
Mikes, 15, 19, 35, 38, 48
Mixing engineer, 27
Mixing tracks, 51
Music-making machines, 1–2
Music Row, 14

Nashville, 6–7, 14–15

Overdubbing, 23, 48, 50

Pearl, Minnie, 7
Percussion, 39, 42, 44, 47
Phasing, 51
Phonograph, 56
Pitch, 39
Presley, Elvis, 7
Pressing machine, 67–68
Producer, 23, 26–27, 31, 46, 51, 74
Punching in, 39

Punching out, 21, 39

Radio station, 11, 47, 73
Record(s)
    care of, 77
    contracts, 26
    45's, 10–11
    grooves in, 59
    made from, 64, 66
    pressing, 64, 67, 72
    profits from, 74
Recording
    for commercials, 50
    "live," 48–49
    for radio, 11, 13
    separate instruments, 15–19, 23
    sessions, 27, 31–47
Recording studio, 13, 15
Reverberation, 53
Rhythm and blues, 6–7
Rock and roll, 7
Rotation, 73

Singles, 10
Song publisher, 11
Song writer, 11, 23
Sound control room, 15, 17, 25, 35
Sound effects, 51–52
Sound engineer, 21, 27, 35, 38
Sound tracks, 21, 23, 25

(84)

Sound waves, 19
Stamper, 63, 67, 74, 77
Stereo, 53
String instruments, 19, 23, 48, 50
Studio manager, 26
Studio musicians, 11, 13, 26–27
Studio room, 15–16
Stylus, 4–5, 56, 58, 60

Tape
    master, 53
    for recording, 21, 53
Tape recorder, 21
Television, and recording music, 11, 13
Tempo, 39
Twenty-four track recording, 21–22, 25

Vocalist
    lead, 27, 31
    recording a, 19, 23, 39, 42–43

About the Author

Lani van Ryzin, author of the popular *Disco* (a Concise Guide) published by Franklin Watts just a little over a year ago, is a former elementary school teacher and is now a freelance writer. Lani lives in Madison, Wisconsin, with her family. Her four teenagers, who have their own band, keep her well informed on what's happening in the music world.

789.9
UAN

789.9
VAN   Van Ryzin, Lani

AUTHOR
Cutting a record in Nashville

TITLE
6.75

789.9
VAN

Van Ryzin, Lani

Cutting a record in Nashville

GOWER MIDDLE SCHOOL
LEARNING CENTER
7941 S. MADISON
BURR RIDGE, IL 60521

DISCARDED